A SHIFTING ROLE:
America and the World (1900-1912)

TITLE LIST

A SHIFTING ROLE:
America and the World (1900-1912)

BY VICTOR SOUTH

MASON CREST

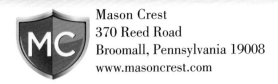

Mason Crest
370 Reed Road
Broomall, Pennsylvania 19008
www.masoncrest.com

Printed and bound in Hashemite Kingdom of Jordan.

First printing
9 8 7 6 5 4 3 2 1

Library of Congress Cataloging-in-Publication Data

South, Victor.
 A shifting role : America and the world, 1900-1912 / by Victor South.
    p. cm. — (How America became America)
 ISBN 978-1-4222-2407-6 (hardcover) — ISBN 978-1-4222-2396-3 (series hardcover) — ISBN 978-1-4222-9317-1 (ebook)
 1. United States—Foreign relations—1901-1909—Juvenile literature. 2. United States—Foreign relations—1909-1913—Juvenile literature. I. Title.
 E756.S68 2013
 327.73009'04—dc23
                                    2012010409

Produced by Harding House Publishing Services, Inc.
www.hardinghousepages.com
Cover design by Torque Advertising + Design.

CONTENTS

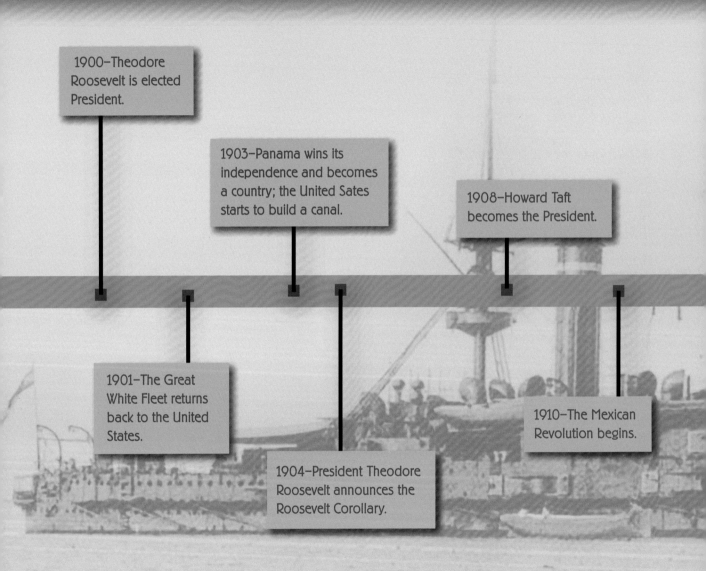

1900–Theodore Roosevelt is elected President.

1903–Panama wins its independence and becomes a country; the United Sates starts to build a canal.

1908–Howard Taft becomes the President.

1901–The Great White Fleet returns back to the United States.

1910–The Mexican Revolution begins.

1904–President Theodore Roosevelt announces the Roosevelt Corollary.

1913–Woodrow Wilson becomes the U.S. President.

1913–Victoriano Huerta becomes the dictator of Mexico.

1916–Mexican bandit Pancho Villa makes his first raids across the border into the United States.

1913–The Wilson Plan is announced, which deals with the political problems in the Dominican Republic.

1914–The Panama Canal is finished.

1912–The U.S. army enters Nicaragua.

Theodore Roosevelt

Chapter One
GROWING POWER

In 1901, sixteen gleaming white ships sailed in a parade seven miles long. President Theodore Roosevelt watched proudly from the deck of another boat.

The ships were coming home from a journey around the world. They had stopped in twenty different ports along the way. They landed on six continents.

All together, the ships were called the "Great White Fleet." It was Teddy Roosevelt's way of telling the world—the United States is a powerful country!

BIGGER AND BIGGER

Of course, people had known about the United States before. But many Americans wanted the United States to have a bigger role in the world. Roosevelt agreed.

Americans wanted the United States to be great. To them, that meant that the country would get bigger. It had already spread from the Atlantic to the Pacific oceans. Where else could it spread? People started looking across the ocean.

If the United States got bigger, it would be more powerful. It could also bring **democracy** and freedom to new people. The United States would really be doing the world a favor. Or at least that's what Americans told themselves.

Democracy is a form of government where the people get to vote for their leaders.

"GREETINGS"

from CALIFORNIA"

A postcard commemorates one of the Great White Fleet.

This is called imperialism. It means that a country builds an empire. The most recent empire was the British Empire. It had included the American colonies. The colonies hadn't liked being part of the British Empire. So they revolted and became the United States.

Not everybody wanted America to build its own empire. Some people thought the United States should mind its own business. It shouldn't try to take over other countries. It should set an example of peace for the rest of the world.

MANIFEST DESTINY

In the 1800s, the United States was just on the East Coast. But there was room to grow. Americans thought that they should spread out over the whole continent. They believed they had a responsibility to bring democracy to people who didn't have it. They thought God wanted them to do that. That idea was called Manifest Destiny. It was one of the reasons that people moved out West and made it all the way to California, Alaska, and Hawaii.

There were also a lot more people in the United States. They needed room to live. They started moving out West, where there was plenty of land. They ignored the fact that Native Americans already lived there.

Roosevelt's campaign speech

Before he was president, Roosevelt worked for the Navy. He had always been ready for war, as long as it meant it could make the United States grow. Now, he especially wanted to make the Navy stronger. A strong fleet of ships would make the United States powerful.

Great Britain had once been the biggest power in the world. Now it was weaker. Other countries were taking over some of their colonies. The United States decided it was time to take Britain's place in the world.

These things are still talked about today. The United States is a very powerful country. How should we use that power? Should the United States run other countries? Is it okay for us to spread democracy? Are we helping other people around the world when we do that? Should our power have a limit?

These are hard questions. In a lot of ways, today's Americans are still facing the same questions that Americans did a hundred years ago, back in the first years of the twentieth century.

THE BRITISH EMPIRE

Britain started getting more powerful during the 1500s, under Queen Elizabeth I. Her explorers traveled all around the world. They claimed land for England everywhere they went. The British ended up owning a lot of land with a lot of things that could make them money. Furs, spices, and slaves all went to Britain. The British created colonies in North America, Africa, India, and other places. The power of the British kept growing for a long time.

Boat entering the Panama Canal in 1915.

Chapter Two
THE PANAMA CANAL

For a long time, there was no easy way to get from the Atlantic to the Pacific Ocean by boat. Not if you were in North or South America. You had to sail all the way to the very southern tip of South America. It was a very, very long journey.

The other option was to take your ships apart. Then you dragged everything across the narrowest part of the Americas. Then you built your ships again.

A GOOD IDEA

Then somebody came up with the idea of a canal. People could build a waterway through that narrowest piece of land. Then ships could sail straight from one ocean to the other without having to travel extra thousands of miles.

The most obvious place to build a canal was in Central America. There were just a few miles of land there that separated the oceans.

Spain had a lot of power in that part of the world. The Spanish started thinking about building a canal. It would help them out a lot.

First, Spain wanted to build it in Nicaragua. But then Nicaragua became a free country. Spain couldn't build the canal because it didn't control the country any more. But Nicaragua could build it.

The United States was also interested in building a canal. They sent a lot of ships around South America. A canal would be useful for trading and for the military.

The first American to think about it was Benjamin Franklin. But the Revolutionary War was going on, so there wasn't any time to think about it. The idea stuck around, though.

The United States looked at a few places to build a canal, with the help of other countries. It looked at Colombia. Then the United States actually started to build a canal in Nicaragua, but didn't get very far.

Meanwhile, the French started building a canal in Panama. But it turned out to be a disaster. There were floods and earthquakes and diseases and accidents. The French gave up. It was too much trouble.

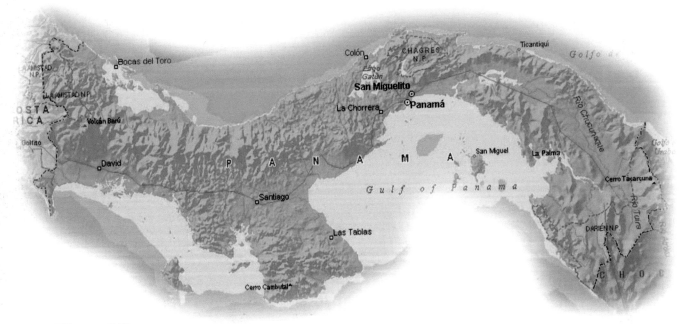

Map of Panama

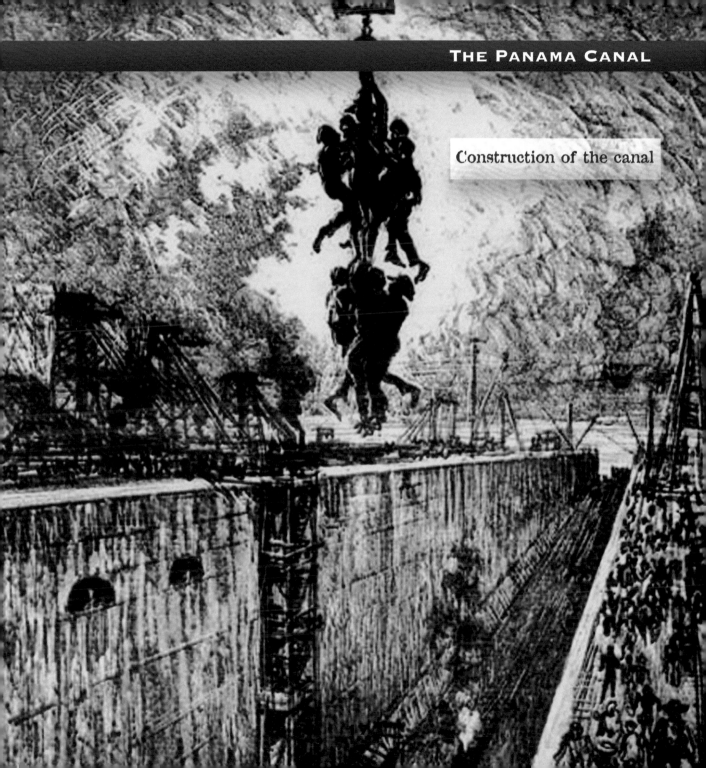

Construction of the canal

BUILDING BEGINS

Finally, the United States was ready to really build a canal. They had time to focus on it now. The problem was, the government still didn't know where it wanted to build.

There were two choices. A canal could be built in Nicaragua. There was a river and a lake that could help builders. They wouldn't have to build as far.

The other choice was in Panama, where the French had already started. Part of the work was already done.

It was a big argument. Panama started looking like it would be cheaper. But there was still one problem: Panama was owned by Colombia. It wasn't its own country.

Colombia was asking for a lot of money from the United States. It didn't just want to let the United States build a canal. It wanted to get something out of it.

Roosevelt never backed down from a challenge. He used to play a game called "obstacle walk." He usually played it with children who came to visit him. The only rule was to get past obstacles by climbing over them. You couldn't go around them.

That's exactly how Roosevelt tackled this problem. He went right over it. He didn't want to pay Colombia. Instead, he would just make Panama into its own country.

Roosevelt watching the building of the Panama Canal

The people who lived in Panama must have been surprised when crews of white men started building a giant ditch through their land.

A boat loading in the Panama Canal

The United States helped Panama revolt. The U.S. Army helped. And Panama became a country in 1903.

Within a month, the United States was in control of a piece of land in Panama. It was called the Canal Zone. It was ten miles wide. The United States could start building.

The deal made a lot of people mad. Not everyone liked what the United States had done. Some Panamanians were angry. They thought the United States had too much control over their country.

Other countries in South America were mad too. Colombia especially didn't like the United States. It had taken away part of its land and people!

But Americans were generally happy. Having a canal would make trading easier. It also showed the world that the United States was powerful.

TROUBLES

Right away, the United States ran into trouble, though. Panama wasn't a very good place to build a canal. France had found that out before. Now the United States would find it out again, the hard way.

The Canal Zone was in the middle of the jungle. It was hot. The people building the canal got sick. Almost six thousand men died. Most of them had diseases like yellow fever or malaria.

But they kept at it. It took years to build the canal. In 1914, it was finally finished. Thanks to the United States and others, the Atlantic and Pacific oceans were linked together.

Panama

21

Vasco Nuñez
de Balboa

VASCO NUÑEZ DE BALBOA

Balboa was a Spanish conquistador (conqueror) during the 1500s. He came to the Americas looking for treasure. He explored northern South America and the Caribbean.

Balboa has quite a story. He didn't find any treasure and he ended up on a Caribbean island called Hispaniola. He didn't have any money left, so he tried farming. He failed.

He and his dog stowed away on a ship to San Sebastian. He eventually made it down to South America again. He established the first European settlement in South America. Then he walked from the settlement all the way to the Pacific Ocean. He crossed jungles and killed natives. He claimed all of that land for Spain.

Balboa was one man who would have benefited from a canal. At one point, he took his ships apart and dragged them through Panama. This was not unusual for explorers during that time.

The Monroe Doctrine

2, 1823

FELLOW-CITIZENS of the ... sentatives ... At the prop... Government, made through t... siding here, a full power an... mitted to the minister of th... to arrange by amicable nego... interests of the two nations... continent. A similar proposal... Majesty to the government of... been acceded to. The gove... has been desirous, by this friendly... great value which they have... friendship of the Emperor and... best understanding with his... which this interest has given... which they may terminate... for asserting, as a... of the United S... by the fr...

...ations existing between the United State... declare that we should consider any a... extend their system to any portion of... gerous to our peace and safety. With... dependencies of any European powe... red and shall not interfere. But with th... have declared their independence and... whose independence we have, on great c... just principles, acknowledged, we could... position for the purpose of oppressing... in any other manner their destiny, by a... in any other light than as the manifestati... disposition toward the United States. In t... new governments and Spain we declare... the time of their recognition, and to th... and shall continue to adhere, provided n... which, in the judgement of the competer... ...nment, shall make a corresponding... ...ted States indispensable to th... ...s in Spain and Portug... ...his important fact n... ...e allied powers... ...le satisfactory t... ...the internal cor... ...ositions may be... ...ion in which all... ...iffer from theirs... ...d surely none mor... ...regard to Europe,... ...the wars which have... ...nevertheless remain... ...internal concerns... ...nment de facto as th... ...ivate friendly relat... ...ns by a frank, firm... ...nces the just clair... ...from none.

Chapter Three
TAKING OVER LATIN AMERICA

Teddy Roosevelt was a President with a lot of character. Some people loved him and some people hated him.

Roosevelt did a lot of good things for the United States. He found ways to control huge companies that hurt other companies. He set aside land for national parks. He helped make food safer in the United States.

But Roosevelt also did some not so good things. He made a lot of other countries mad. He believed that Central and South America weren't as good as the United States. He thought the United States had the right to control the people who lived there. And he wasn't afraid to use that right.

Roosevelt liked to say "Speak softly and carry a big stick." He meant that you shouldn't get angry and you should be friendly—but you should also be willing to use your strength to fight enemies.

Roosevelt didn't speak very softly. He did carry a big stick, though. And he wasn't afraid to use it.

THE ROOSEVELT COROLLARY

Before Roosevelt's time, the United States wanted to keep Europe out of this part of the world. President James Monroe warned Europe not to do anything in the Western Hemisphere.

HEMISPHERES

If we looked at our planet from outer space, it would look like a huge blue ball. If we cut the ball in half from top to bottom, we would have hemispheres. "Hemi" means half, and a sphere is round—so a hemisphere is half of something round. The Earth's Eastern Hemisphere has Africa, Australia, Europe, and Asia. People who come from this part of the world sometimes call it the "Old World." The Western Hemisphere has what today we call the "Americas." Once they found out it was there, people in the Eastern Hemisphere called the Western Hemisphere the "New World." But it wasn't new to the millions of people who had lived there for thousands of years!

Today, we have given labels to the Western Hemisphere based on the countries that are there. To the north is Alaska, part of the United States of America. Below that is Canada, and then the United States. Below that is Mexico. These three nations—Canada, the United States, and Mexico—are all part of the continent we call North America.

Mexico, though part of North America, is also part of Latin America. Latin America is made up of the nations that begin with Mexico and reach to the southern tip of South America. Spanish-speaking Europeans settled these countries. People who spoke Portuguese settled Brazil in South America.

South of North America is a narrow section of land called Central America. And still further south is South America. There are many countries in Central and South America.

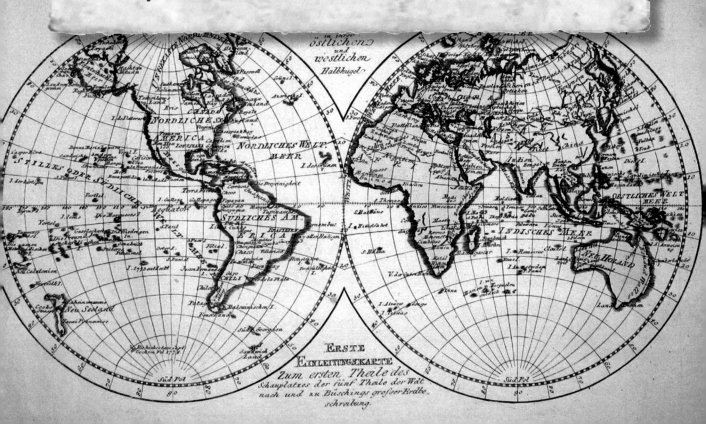

THE MONROE DOCTRINE

The Monroe Doctrine was created in 1823. The president at the time was James Monroe. It was a big turning point in how the United States dealt with the outside world.

The Doctrine said that the United States didn't want Europe interfering with North or South America. The United States would have to use its military if that happened. It also said that the United States wouldn't interfere with Europe.

The United States wanted to have all the power in North and South America. The ideas in the Monroe Doctrine lasted a very long time. They lasted over 200 years! Later presidents would use it to explain American actions. But nobody ever asked Latin American countries what they thought.

If a European country did, the United States would see it as war. That was called the Monroe Doctrine.

Roosevelt added on his own words. He added the Roosevelt **Corollary**. It said that the United States had the right to keep the peace in the Americas. It basically said that

A **corollary** is a statement that's based on an earlier fact. So the Roosevelt Corollary was based on the Monroe Doctrine.

the United States was the boss in all of the Americas. As long as the United States could keep the peace, there was no reason for Europe to come over.

Where did the Corollary come from? It started because of some things that happened in the Dominican Republic. That's an island in the Caribbean.

A man named General Ulises Heureaux became the president of the Dominican Republic in 1882. People liked him at first.

Then he became a **dictator**. He didn't give people any freedom. He killed people. He made the country poor and he owed a lot of money to other countries.

The United States could lose a lot of money based on what the Dominican Republic did. The United States decided this was a reason to get involved in the Dominican Republic.

Then Roosevelt realized it was a reason to get involved in more countries. He didn't want other dictators taking over. The United States could keep things calm. And they could show the world that they were the most powerful country around.

NICARAGUA

Meanwhile, a revolution was happening in Nicaragua. The country had a dictator named José Santos Zelaya.

The United States didn't like Zelaya. He was anti-American. He also was trying to control his neighbors. The United States wanted to be the only powerful country in the area.

Zelaya also had ties to Europe. He got loans from banks in Europe. The United States didn't like that either. Roosevelt wanted Europe out of the Western Hemisphere.

A **dictator** is a ruler that has all the power in a country. He can do anything he wants. Dictators are often cruel.

SEÑOR DON ADOLFO DIAZ,
President of the Republic of Nicaragua.

Nicaraguans didn't like Zelaya much either. In 1909, some of them took over part of the country. The United States helped. But Zelaya fought back. He captured some rebels and killed them.

The rebels eventually won. Adolfo Díaz became the president. The United States agreed to help him on one condition. He had to cut ties with Europe. He had to look to the United States for help.

The United States grew more and more powerful in Nicaragua. It took over its trade. It controlled the president.

Eventually, the United States military arrived. Zelaya's supporters were trying to take over again. The United States sent warships and Marines. The Marines stayed after the conflict. The United States was there to stay.

HAITI

Haiti was another country where the United States had a lot of power in. Haiti is part of an island in the Caribbean. The Dominican Republic is on the other half of the island.

Haiti used to be a French colony. Slaves revolted and made Haiti a country in 1804. For a while, Haiti ruled itself. The people of Haiti didn't want other countries coming in.

By 1900, there were some Europeans who lived in Haiti's capital. They were mostly Germans and French. A lot of them sold Haitian coffee to other countries.

France offered to help Haiti out with its money problems. The United States didn't like that at all. Remember, it wanted to keep Europe out of the Americas.

Haiti's coat
of arms

The Chinese government needed to borrow money from other countries to create a railroad.

The United States started thinking more about Haiti. Eventually, it helped a new president get elected in Haiti. The president was controlled by the United States. And Haiti became another country where the United States had a lot of power.

WORLDWIDE

Mostly the United States was thinking about getting more power in Latin America. Roosevelt was very interested in controlling other countries in Central and South America.

But there was still the rest of the world. The United States wanted to be a world power. It set its sights on other countries too.

European countries had been the most powerful ones for a long time. Now the United States wanted to be the most powerful. So the United States tried to get rid of European influence anywhere they found it.

China was yet another place where Europe was involved. The Chinese government got some loans from the Germans, British, and French. The money was for a railroad.

Again, the United States didn't like that. A group of American bankers offered to give China money instead.

China had two offers: the Europeans or the Americans. It went with the Europeans.

The United States put some pressure on China. The U.S. President sent a note to the leader of China. He let him know that the United States really wanted to give them money. China gave in.

The United States was gaining power through money. It was called "Dollar Diplomacy." Instead of just using the Army to control other countries, the United States was using money.

William Howard Taft

WILLIAM HOWARD TAFT

William Howard Taft was the twenty-seventh President. He was elected after Teddy Roosevelt in 1908.

First, Taft was the Secretary of War under Roosevelt. He knew that Roosevelt wanted him to be the next President. Roosevelt was a popular President. People would vote for the man he wanted to come next.

Taft won the 1908 election easily. Then he had to actually lead the country. He focused a lot on what was going on in Latin America. He pretty much continued Roosevelt's ideas and actions.

He wasn't very well-liked as a President. Lots of people disagreed with him. He only served one term as President. He later became the head of the Supreme Court. He's the only person to have both been both the President and the Chief Justice on the Supreme Court.

Woodrow Wilson

Chapter Four
PRESIDENT WILSON

Woodrow Wilson was elected as the President in 1913. Changes were happening in Washington, D.C.

The United States kept getting stronger. It still wanted a presence all over the world. Wilson generally went along with the ideas of the two Presidents who had come before him. One of the places where Wilson got involved was Mexico.

BAD GOVERNMENT

The United States and Mexico share a border. That doesn't mean they always get along. In the 1800s, the United States took a lot of land away from Mexico. The United States got bigger. Mexico got smaller.

By the end of the 1800s, the two countries were at peace, though. Porfirio Díaz was Mexico's leader. He wasn't a very good leader for the average Mexican. He treated the Mexican Natives badly. He gave away Mexican land. He also borrowed a lot of money from other countries.

Díaz made a lot of money for himself. He didn't let his people have much of it. Mexicans were unhappy.

In 1910, a **revolution** broke out. The poor and the **middle class** fought against the president. They won.

The rebels set up Francisco Madero as the president. But soon, the winners of the revolution were fighting with each other. They couldn't agree on how to run the government.

All those countries that had given Mexico money were worried. What would happen?

More changes were coming soon. Some people were unhappy with Madero. They wanted yet a different government. Those people got together. They chose Victoriano Huerta as their new president. Then they killed Madero and made Huerta Mexico's leader in 1913.

That was where President Wilson came in. He became President in the United States at the same time Huerta did in Mexico. Wilson refused to say that Huerta's government was real. Wilson thought that Huerta could easily become a dictator. Wilson wanted the people that had supported Madero to lead Mexico instead.

Soon, Huerta declared himself as a dictator. He had a lot of power. What's more, Wilson thought that Europeans were helping Huerta. President Wilson wouldn't stand for that. Pretty soon, the United States invaded Mexico.

WAR IN MEXICO

Now there was fighting between Americans and Mexicans. Soldiers fought and died.

Huerta was in trouble. People who disagreed with him persuaded him to leave. But by now, the United States was committed to fighting. Americans couldn't back down now.

A **revolution** is when the people fight to get rid of the government.

The **middle class** are the people who are neither very rich nor very poor.

The Americans eventually decided to support a man named Pancho Villa. He was on their side. He was connected to another man named Emiliano Zapata.

Pancho Villa

At first, the United States and Villa worked together. Then things changed. The United States decided to finally officially recognize the Mexican government. Villa was angry.

He crossed into the United States and killed Americans. The United States struck back. They sent an army general to find him.

The general never found Villa. But the search grew and grew. Warships and border patrols got involved.

The whole thing was a mess. It had long-lasting effects on the United States and on Mexico. In Mexico, people didn't like the United States anymore. Because of the United States, Mexicans had died and the country was in chaos. Mexicans didn't trust the United States.

THE CARIBBEAN

Mexico wasn't the only place with trouble for President Wilson. The Caribbean had problems too. Presidents Roosevelt and Taft had already gotten the United States involved in the area.

In 1913, the Dominican Republic was still having problems. So the United States came up with the "Wilson Plan." The plan called for elections in the Dominican Republic run by Americans. The United States would help the Dominicans with their money problems. And the United States military would run the Dominican army.

REVOLUTIONARY HEROES

Pancho Villa and Emiliano Zapata are considered to be heroes by a lot of people. Villa is particularly famous.

Villa was born in Durango, Mexico. He lived on a ranch until he was 16. Then he shot his boss's son. He ran away to avoid getting in trouble. He became a miner and stole cattle for a living. He got bored, so he started robbing banks.

Villa got together a group of men. Together they were outlaws. The Mexican government was looking for him. But poor people loved him. He was a hero for them. He stole from the rich and gave to the poor. He was a Mexican Robin Hood.

Villa and his gang fought for Francisco Madero. They wanted him to be president. Americans came to fight with them.

Americans couldn't get enough of Pancho Villa. He was in the newspaper all the time. Filmmakers came to Mexico to make movies about him.

Zapata was born in Morelos, Mexico. He became a local leader in his town. He started growing an army. It grew bigger and bigger and it eventually overthrew Porfirio Díaz. Later, his army fought against Victoriano Huerta.

Zapata wanted to give back the land to ordinary people. His motto was *"Tierra y libertad"* ("Land and liberty"). He fought for people's rights for many years, until his death.

Pancho Villa and others

The Dominicans accepted. They didn't have a lot of choice. The Wilson Plan didn't really work, though. The Dominican president it helped elect was weak. He had a breakdown and the government fell apart.

The United States finally just invaded the Dominican Republic. America made its own military government in that country for almost ten years.

Meanwhile, in another part of the Caribbean, the United States bought the Virgin Islands. These were a bunch of small islands owned by Denmark. The United States had wanted the Virgin Islands for a long time. They were a good place for military reasons.

Back in 1866, the United States and Denmark had talked about the islands. Nothing had ever really happened, though. Not much happened for fifty more years.

Eventually, Denmark sold the Virgin Island to the United States. It still owns them today.

THE PHILIPPINES

The Philippines are a group of islands on the other side of the world. The United States had gained control over the Philippines in 1898. Spain had owned them before that. Then when Spain lost the Spanish-American War, the United States took over the Philippines.

President Wilson decided to let the people from the Philippines have more of a say in their country. He decided to give them **independence**—but only when their government was **stable**. This was a step in a different direction. Mostly the United States was

Flag of the Phillippines

Independence means freedom from outside control.

Stable means that something is steady. It doesn't change a lot.

trying to have more control over countries. In the Philippines, though, Americans were trying to give up control.

A lot was going on during this time. America was getting bigger. It was figuring out how to use its new power.

But soon Americans would have other things to worry about. The United States would have to focus on Europe for a while. World War I was about to begin.

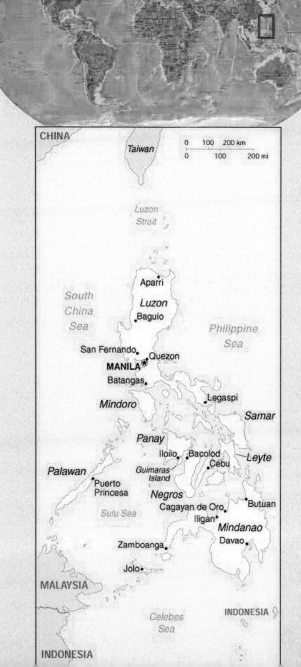

Map of the Phillippines

43

FIND OUT MORE

In Books

Harness, Cheryl. *The Remarkable Rough-Riding Life of Theodore Roosevelt and the Rise of Empire America.* Washington, D.C.: National Geographic Children's Books, 2007.

Mann, Elizabeth. *The Panama Canal.* New York: Mikaya Press, 2006.

Mara, Will. *Theodore Roosevelt.* Danbury, Conn.: Children's Press, 2007.

Stein, R. Conrad. *The Mexican Revolution: 1910-1920.* New Delhi, India: New Discovery, 1994.

On the Internet

Mexican Revolution
www.mexconnect.com/articles/2824-the-mexican-revolution-1910

Panama Canal
www.pancanal.com/eng

Theodore Roosevelt Association
www.theodoreroosevelt.org

The White House
www.whitehouse.gov/about/presidents

INDEX

ABOUT THE AUTHOR

Victor South is a freelance author from New York State. He grew up reading the stories that helped shape America. He is excited about the opportunity to share these stories with a new generation of children.

ABOUT THE CONSULTANT

Dr. Jack N. Rakove is a professor of history and American studies at Stanford University, where he is director of American studies. The winner of the 1997 Pulitzer Prize in history, Dr. Rakove is the author of *The Unfinished Election of 2000*, *Constitutional Culture and Democratic Rule*, and *James Madison and the Creation of the American Republic*. He is also the president of the Society for the History of the Early American Republic.